Eva

FOOD
Vibes

A NEW WAY FOR YOU TO ENJOY WHAT TO EAT FOR HOW YOU FEEL THROUGH FOOD, RELAXATION AND AYURVEDA

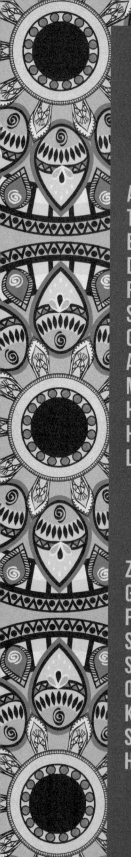

Table Of Content

Revitalizing Time   53

Easy to make

Sweet

~~~~~~~~~~

Sensation

Apricot Granola Bars

 14 servings 15 minutes 🍲 20 minutes

Ingredients

1 cup of honey
¼ cup of dark brown sugar
½ tsp of kosher salt
1 tsp of vanilla extract
1 cup of sliced almonds
1 cup of diced dried apricots
¼ cup of oat bran
½ cup of shredded sweetened coconut

¼ cup of ground flaxseed
1 ¼ cups of rolled oats
1 ½ cups of rice crisps
1 tbsp of sesame seeds
¾ tsp of ginger
¾ tsp of cinnamon

Equipments

1 qt. Saucepan
Stand Mixer

Directions

1. Preheat the oven to 350 degrees Fahrenheit. Cook and spray gently with the spray and set aside the 8 by 11-inch sheet pan.
2. Bring the honey, dark brown sugar, and salt to a boil in a saucepan and then reduce the heat and stir until the sugar is dissolved. To mix, add the vanilla and whisk.
3. Attach the mixture attached to a paddle attachment to the stand mixer.
4. In a medium-sized cup, mix the nuts, apricots, oat bran, coconut, flaxseed, oats, crepes, sesame, ginger, and cinnamon.
5. Add the mixture to the mixture and blend until the wet and dry ingredients come together at medium speed.
6. To the prepared pan, move the granola mixture and spread uniformly, press with a spatula to make the surface about 1 inch thick.
7. Bake the tray until the edges and tops are very light golden brown, for 18 to 20 minutes.
8. Cool for about an hour to room temperature. For fast cutting, refrigerate the bars for a minimum of 2 hours.
9. Cut the bars into 4-inch bars of 1.5 inches or the necessary size.

Toasted Oatmeal

 1 servings    10 minutes   30 minutes

Ingredients

1 tbsp of unsalted butter
1 cup of Irish, Scottish, or any steel-cut oatmeal
Pinch coarse salt
Infused Honey
Stewed Fruit

Directions

1. Melt butter over medium heat in a big heavy saucepan.
2. Add the oats and toast for about 4 minutes, tossing and turning the oats until the oatmeal is browned and fragrant.
3. Apply 4 cups of salt and water and bring it to a boil.
4. Cook until much of the water has evaporated and the oatmeal is soft, around 30 minutes for the Irish oatmeal and 10 minutes for the old-fashioned rolled oats.
5. Reduce to simmer. With the toppings of your preference, serve sweet.

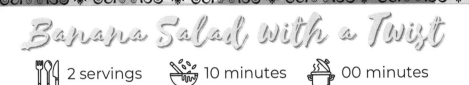

Banana Salad with a Twist

🍴 2 servings   🥗 10 minutes   🍲 00 minutes

Ingredients

1 2 ripe bananas
2 ripe tomatoes
1 tbsp of chopped fresh cilantro
4 fresh chopped mint leaves
2 tsp of lemon juice
1/2 tsp of roasted, cumin powder
1/4 tsp of red chili powder
2 tsp of sugar powder
4 pinch black salt
1/4 tsp of salt

Directions

1. Save aside half of the coriander for garnish.
2. Chop the bananas, whisk in the lemon juice and gently mix.
3. To chop the tomatoes, combine all the other components.
4. Add the bananas.
5. Toss gently with a flat spoon.
6. Chill if needed.
7. Leftover cilantro garnish. Merely serve.

Dried Fig and Nut Bars

 36 servings    60 minutes   35 minutes

Ingredients

- 1 cup whole, toasted, skinned hazelnuts (about 5 ounces)
- 1 cup whole, toasted almonds (about 5 ounces)
- 2/3 cup all-purpose flour
- 2 tablespoons unsweetened cocoa powder
- 2 1/4 teaspoons finely grated orange zest (from 1 medium orange)
- 2 teaspoons fennel seeds, lightly crushed
- 1/2 teaspoon ground cinnamon
- 1/8 teaspoon ground cloves
- 8 ounces dried black Mission figs, stemmed and thinly sliced (about 1 1/2 cups)
- 2/3 cup granulated sugar
- 1/2 cup honey

1. Heat the oven to 300°F.
2. Coarsely chop hazelnuts and almonds and set them aside.
3. Coat a 10-inch springform pan with butter and flour and set aside.
4. Stir together flour, cocoa powder, orange zest, fennel seeds, cinnamon, and cloves in a large bowl until evenly mixed.
5. Add nuts and figs and stir to coat.
6. In a small saucepan, stir together sugar and honey and place over low heat. Increase heat to medium and cook, without stirring, until the mixture reaches 245°F on a candy thermometer for about 6 minutes.
7. Immediately pour over nut mixture and, working quickly, stir until dry ingredients are coated (the mixture will be very thick).
8. Transfer to the prepared pan and, with moistened fingers, press evenly into the pan.
9. Bake until mixture has puffed slightly and has a toasty aroma, about 35 minutes. (The mixture will be soft and tacky to the touch.)
10. Transfer to a rack to cool to room temperature, at least 1 hour.
11. Remove from the pan and cut horizontally into thirds, then cut each third into 1/2-inch-thick bars (you should have about 36 bars).

Rice pudding with Candied Ginger Cinnamon

🍴 12 servings   🍚 10 minutes   🍲 45 minutes

Ingredients

1 1/2 cups of water
3/4 cup of basmati rice
1/4 tsp of sea salt
3 cups of whole milk
1 cup of heavy whipping cream
1/2 cup of sugar
1/2 vanilla bean split lengthwise
1 tsp of ground cinnamon
4 tbsp of chopped candied ginger

Directions

1. Simmer 1 1/2 cups of water, rice, and salt over medium-high heat in a strong, large saucepan. Decrease the heat to a low level; cover.
2. Simmer for about 10 minutes, before the water is absorbed. Incorporate milk, cream, and sugar.
3. Scrape the vanilla bean into the seeds; add the bean or add the vanilla extract and the cinnamon. Increase heat to medium; cook uncovered until rice is tender and the mixture thickens slightly, stirring occasionally, to a smooth, creamy texture, around 35 minutes. If the blend appears to be runny, not to worry, it will thicken as it cools down.
4. Remove the pudding from the heat and discard, if used, the vanilla bean. Incorporate candied ginger.
5. To Serve: Split the pudding into 8 small bowls equally.
6. Serve hot or press the plastic wrap directly onto each pudding surface and cool thoroughly.

Steel-Cut Oatmeal with Fruit

 4 servings   15 minutes   🍲 30 minutes

Ingredients

2 cups of water
2 cups of low-fat milk
¼ tsp of salt
1 cup of steel-cut oats
1 tsp of unsalted butter
2 to 4 tbsps of dried fruit, such as raisins, chopped dried apricots, dried cranberries
1 to 2 tsp of maple syrup, agave syrup, honey, or brown sugar
Fresh fruit

Directions

1. In a big, heavy saucepan, mix the water, milk, and salt, and bring it to a boil. Apply the oats slowly, stirring continuously. Reduce the heat to medium, cover, and simmer for 15 minutes, occasionally stirring with a wooden spoon.
2. Stir in the honey, sweetener, and dried fruit. Cover and continue to simmer for another 10 to 15 minutes, stirring regularly, until the oats are soft and the mixture is creamy to prevent the cereal from sticking to the bottom of the pan.
3. Serve, if necessary, with added fruit stirred in, or cool and reheat as necessary.

1. Or as follows, freeze:
2. Put a line of plastic-wrapped ice cube trays. Fill each cube with oatmeal, cover, and freeze with plastic wrap. Remove the cubes from the ice tray until the solid has frozen and frozen them in a plastic bag. In the defrost environment, thaw three or four cubes in a microwave for each component. When needed, add additional warm milk.

Golden Pancakes

🍴 2 servings   🥣 5 minutes   🍲 5 minutes

Ingredients

1 1/2 cups all purpose flour
3 Tbsp of granulated sugar
2 tsp of baking powder
1/2 tsp of baking soda
1/2 of tsp salt
1 cup of milk
2 large eggs
3 Tbsp of canola oil

Directions

1. Heat the electric grid to 325 ° F (160 ° C).
2. Sift the flour, sugar, baking powder, baking soda, and salt together in a medium cup.
3. In a separate cup, whisk together the milk, eggs, and canola oil.
4. Into the dry mixture, pour the wet ingredients and stir until mixed. Do not over-mix.
5. Take an electrical grid of canola oil and oil.
6. Pour 1/4 cup (60 mL) batter onto a griddle to make pancakes. Cook for approximately 1 1/2 minutes on each side (depending on size).

Apple Cinnamon Oatmeal

🍴 4 servings   🥣 5 minutes   🍲 10 minutes

1 tbsp of coconut oil
1 large 2 small apple, cutted into small chunks
½ tsp of cinnamon
Pinch of nutmeg
¼ cup of pecans or walnuts
1 cup of gluten-free ground oats
2 cups of unsweetened almond milk
1 tsp of chia seeds optional
1 tbsp of maple syrup
¼ cup of pomegranate seeds as garnish

Directions

1. Heat the coconut oil over medium heat in a medium-sized saucepan.
2. Put the apples in and saute for 2-3 minutes.
3. Stir in the nutmeg and cinnamon.
4. Add (if using) the pecans, peas, almond milk, and chia seeds.
5. Stir it and let it steam, constantly stirring for 5-7 minutes during the cooking process.
6. Ladle the pomegranate seeds (or other fruit) and nuts into bowls and top them off.
7. Just serve.

Mango Cake

 2 servings   15 minutes   25 minutes

Ingredients

1 1/2 Cup whole wheat flour
1/2 Cup of Mango Puree
1/4 Cup of Milk
1/2 Cup of Sugar
4 Tbsp of Coconut oil
1/2 Tsp of Vanilla Extract
1 Tsp of Baking Powder
1/2 Tsp of Baking Soda
Salt a pinch

Directions

1. 350 degrees F. Preheated oven.
2. In a cup, look for whole wheat flour, baking powder, baking soda, and salt.
3. Place the coconut oil and sugar in another bowl and blend until the sugar dissolves. Mix well with the vanilla essence, the mango purée, then.
4. Only add milk.
5. Then add the flour slowly until it is thoroughly mixed with all the flour mixture.
6. The Bata is going to be thicker.
7. Place the cake in a frying pan and bake for 25-30 minutes in a preheated oven or until the toothpaste is clean.
8. Serve in airtight containers or clip wrappers.
9. For up to a week it can be kept in the refrigerator.

Honey Pistachio Pancakes

🍴 2 servings   🥣 15 minutes   🍲 25 minutes

Ingredients

3/4 cup of milk
4 tbsps of separated butter
3/4 cup of (94 grams) all purpose flour
1 1/2 cups of pistachios
2 tsps of baking powder
1/2 tsp of salt

1 tsp of vanilla extract
1 large egg
3 tbsps of honey
6 wonton wrappers6 wonton wrappers
1 tbsp of dark brown sugar

1. In the food processor, place one cup of pesto. Process before, as in most sequences, you find some small sections of sand.
2. Process up to a medium-large portion of the remaining 1/2 cup. These are delivered in pancakes
3. Heat the milk and 2 tbsps of butter until melted, over low heat. Remove from the fire and leave it for a few minutes to cool.
4. In a big bowl , mix the first batch of flour, baking powder , salt and refined pesto.
5. Add the egg, vanilla, milk, butter mixture, and honey to a medium cup. Until combined, whisk.
6. Add the liquid ingredients to the dry ingredients and stir until they are combined. This is fine if you are still ambitious. Glue the mixture like a pancake. Add some more milk at once if the paste is too thick.
7. Spray a small amount of butter with cooking spray or grease in a non-stick pan. I heat my pan over medium low heat and adjust it to low once the pancakes are added.
8. In medium-sized circles, add your bata and flip over the pancakes as the bubbles begin to appear. Cook for a few more minutes.
9. Your wontons are prepared while preparing pancakes.
10. Melt the remaining two tbsps of butter and apply dark brown sugar to the mixture.
11. With the mixture, clean all sides of the Wanton wrapper.
12. Place the wontons in a frying pan over medium heat and cook on both sides until brown. When you remove them from the sun, these crops will expand. Break them into tiny bits.
13. To assemble your pancakes, add 1-2 tsps of honey to the pancakes and top with crushed cake and toasted wrappers.

Honey Corn Cake

 12 servings   15 minutes   50 minutes

Ingredients

1 cup of corn flour
½ cup of fine cornmeal
½ cup of all-purpose unbleached flour
1 tbsp of baking powder
½ cup of softened unsalted butter
1 ½ cups of brown sugar
3 eggs
1 cup of milk
¼ cup of softenedunsalted butter
½ cup of honey

Directions

1. Preheat the oven to 180 degrees centigrade (350 degrees Fahrenheit) place the rack in the middle with a 20 centimeter (8 inches) square baking pan of butter. Line the pan with a strip of parchment paper, letting it hang on both sides.
2. In a bowl, combine cornflour, cornmeal, flour, and baking powder. Set aside.
3. In another bowl, whisk together the butter and brown sugar. Add the eggs at once and beat until smooth. Periodically add the dried ingredients to the milk at low speed in the prepared pan.
4. Bake for about 50 minutes or until the toothpick is cooked through the middle of the cake.
5. Meanwhile, in a small saucepan, melt the butter and honey just above the entire surface of the cake from the oven. Allow the pan to cool completely. Unmolded and cut into squares. Serve with whipped cream and berries.

Lemon Snack Cakes

 4 servings   20 minutes   50 minutes

Ingredients

FOR LEMON CAKE

2 cups of Cake Flour
1 1/4 cups of Sugar
1 tbsp of Baking Powder
1 tsp of Salt
1 tsp of Lemon Zest
7 Eggs separated
1/2 cup of Unsalted Butter melted
1/2 cup of Milk
1/4 cup of Lemon Juice

FOR LEMON CREME

7.5 oz Jar of Marshmallow Creme
1/2 cup of Unsalted Butter
2 tsps of Lemon Juice
1 tsp of Lemon Zest

FOR LEMON FROSTING

1/2 cup of Unsalted Butter
2 cups of Confectioners Sugar
2 tsps of Lemon Juice

Directions

FOR LEMON CAKE

1. Heat the oven to 176.667 degrees C.
2. Spray a 9x9 "square baking pan with nonstick spray
3. Combine the salt, baking powder, 1 cup of sugar, and flour with a fork in a dish.
4. In another cup, shake for 5-7 minutes until the crumbs are thick and pale using egg yolks and a mixture.
5. Gently add the flour mixture, mixing with butter and lemon juice. Eventually, mix in the lemon zest
6. Beat the egg whites in another bowl until rigid.
7. Carefully fold the egg whites into 2-3 installments using a spatula on the egg whites. To invalidate the egg whites, use circular motions
8. Pour the batter into the prepared pan and bake until golden brown for about 20-30 minutes.
9. Remove from oven and place on top of baking rack for 20 minutes
10. Invert the pan into the baking rack and unmold
11. Absolutely cool cake
12. Cover the cooled cake in plastic and leave it for quick cutting and stuffing for a few hours.

FOR LEMON CREME

1. Mix all ingredients together until fluffy
2. In a piping jar, spoon the cream and snip the bottom
3. Remove the cake and break it into tiny baking cakes from the fridge.
4. With a knife, cut 3 deep slits on the surface of the cake to make sure you have wide pockets for cracks.
5. Keep piping bags in every pocket and stuffed pastries
6. Clean the tops of the cakes and cool them while you freeze.

LEMON FROSTING

1. In a bowl, mix the butter, lemon juice, and sugar.
2. Mix until nice and smooth at a medium pace.
3. Place the fry in a piping bag with a wide icing tip
4. Piping the frosting over the top slowly
5. Enjoy!

AYURVEDA

Quick to make
Regenerating
Breaks

Zucchini Bread Muffins

🍴 12 servings   🥣 15 minutes   🍲 20 minutes

Ingredients

1 1/2 cups of flour
1 cup of sugar
1 tsp of cinnamon
½ tsp of baking powder
½ tsp of baking soda
½ tsp of salt
2 large eggs
½ cup of oil
1 tsp of vanilla
2 cup of finely grated unpeeled zucchini

Directions

1. Place the muffin tin in a preheated oven at 350 degrees and line it with a graph or paper.
2. Whisk the flour, sugar, cinnamon, baking powder, baking soda, and salt in a big bowl.
3. In the grease, fry the eggs, then stir in the vanilla. In the dry ingredients, stir the wet ingredients until they are scarcely mixed (the mixture will be very thick and a little dry).
4. When it is incorporated, fold the zucchini into the layer.
5. Tins of muffins are 3/4 loaded.
6. Bake until the toothpick is clean, for 20-22 minutes.
7. Place in a separate plastic wrap at room temperature or an airtight jar for 5 days and refrigerate for up to 3 weeks. Serve or pop them in the microwave for a few seconds at room temperature and pound them with some butter.

Garlic Parmesan Shortbread

 12 servings  10 minutes   25 minutes

Ingredients

1 cup of corn meal
1 cup of flour
⅓ cup of sugar
1 Tsp of baking powder
½ tsp of salt
2 beaten eggs
1 cup of buttermilk
3 Tbsp of Chef Shamy Garlic Butter
1 cup of shredded Parmesan cheese

Directions

1. 375 degrees Fahrenheit from the preheated oven
2. Add the cornmeal, flour, sugar, baking powder, and salt to a large mixing bowl.
3. In a separate mixing bowl, blend the beaten eggs, buttermilk, and melted garlic butter.
4. Fold the moist ingredients into the dry ingredients gently.
5. To mix, add the parmesan cheese and whisk.
6. Bata in a 9x9 baking dish grilled.
7. Bake for 20-25 minutes at 375 ° F until the toothpick in the center is clean.
8. Let cool, then cut into 12 bits.
9. Serve with broth, pepper, and extra garlic butter.

Fennel and Orange Salad with Toasted Pistachios

 4 servings 20 minutes 🍲 00 minutes

Ingredients

2 peeled, quartered, thinly sliced and navel oranges

1 small bulb fennel, quartered, cored, and very thinly cut crosswise

1 cup of very thinly sliced radishes or diced peeled jicama

¼ cup of coarsely chopped fresh cilantro

2 tbsps of extra-virgin olive oil or pistachio oil

1 tbsp plus 1 tsp of lime juice

¼ tsp of salt

Freshly ground pepper

6 tbsps of toasted and chopped shelled salted pistachio nuts

Directions

1. In a bowl, mix the orange slices, fennel, radish, coriander leaves, oil, lime juice, salt and pepper.
2. Sprinkle the nuts softly over the salad, just before serving the toss, to blend.

Sesame Crunch Bars

 6 servings   5 minutes   10-30 minutes

Ingredients

3/4 cup of raw sesame seeds
1/2 cup of maple syrup
Pinch salt

Directions

- Preheat the oven to 325 when the oven process is done.
- Toast the sesame seeds until fragrant and golden.
- Stovetop method: Add maple syrup and salt.
- Cook until the maple syrup is cooked, continually stirring, for about 3-5 minutes.
- Mix the mixture on a packed baking mat or terracotta paper sprayed with cooking spray.
- To roll and flatten uniformly, put a piece of parchment paper on top (also sprayed with cooking spray) and use a rolling pin when the mixture is a little rough but slightly soft, split.

OVEN METHOD
- Combine the ingredients and create a double-lined leather paper baking sheet on the top and aluminum foil with the paper to ensure the lip is the bottom layer. Two layers are required because the mixture will leak under the first layer, and this will cover your baking sheet.
- Bake for 30 minutes at 325.
- When the mixture is a little rough but a little soft, split.

Spring Onion Curry

 2 servings   10 minutes   🍲 15 minutes

Ingredients

1 bunch of spring Onions
1 Onion
2 Tomato
2 of green chilies
1/2 of Kalonji or Onion Seeds
1 tsp Ginger garlic paste
2 tsp coriander powder

1 tsp of Red chili powder
1/2 tsp of Turmeric powder
1 tsp of garam masala powder
Salt
1 tsp of oil

Directions

1. Wash the bunch of spring onions and detach the white onion bulbs from the green ones. Separately, cut the white and green pieces.
2. Cut and set aside the onion, tomato, and green pepper.
3. Heat the oil in a pan.
4. Add the kalonji and add the dried white portion of the spring onion when cooked, and fry on low heat for ½ minute.
5. Reduce the flame, add the chopped onion, and fry until it tastes like onion.
6. Now add a paste of ginger garlic and cook for a minute.
7. Add the chopped green peppers, tomatoes, salt, and cook until the tomatoes are soft, for 3-4 minutes.
8. Mix well with chili powder, turmeric powder, and coriander powder. Add 3-4 tbsps of water and cook until the crude odor disappears for 2 minutes.
9. Add the chopped green portion of the spring onion, mix well until wet, and then cook for 2-3 minutes.
10. Mix well, close the pan with an idacana and cook for 4-5 minutes until the raw flavor disappears, and the volume of gravy is a little thicker.
11. Add 1/4 cup of water (approximately).
12. Apply the hot spice powder and blend to taste well.
13. With a fork, serve hot.

Okra Stir Fry

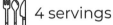 4 servings  10 minutes   20minutes

Ingredients

2 tbsps of GrapeOla Grape Seed oil
1 diced medium onion
2 tsps minced garlic
1 tsp minced ginger
1 green sliced lengthwise chili
1 cup of green peas
¼ cup of toasted cashews
2 tbsps of chopped fresh mint
1 cup of Royal Basmati Rice
1 ¾ cups of water
1 star anise
1 cinnamon stick
3 green cardamom pods
2 tsps of cumin seeds
1 bay leaf
Salt and pepper

Directions

1. Heat oil over medium heat in a medium saute pan with a close-fitting lid.
2. Add the onion and sauté until soft, 3 to 5 minutes.
3. To combine, add garlic, ginger, chili, peas, and cashews and stir.
4. Mint, rice, water, and spices are added. Just bring it to a boil. Cook for 15 minutes or until water is absorbed.
5. Reduce heat to boil and cover.

Kitchari

🍴 4 servings   🍚 5 minutes   🍲 35 minutes

Ingredients

1/2 cup moong dal, mung beans divided
1/2 cup Basmati rice
4 cups water
1 tbsp ghee, coconut oil
1 tsp cumin seeds
1/2 tsp minced fresh ginger, or a pinch of ground ginger powder
1/4 tsp ground turmeric
1 tsp sea salt
1/4 tsp black pepper

FOR GARNISH

1/2 cup of chopped fresh cilantro
slices of lime or lemon

Directions

1. Combine the rice and Moong Dal in a medium dish. To cover the mixture, pour in enough water and soak for 15 minutes.
2. Pour the mixture into a fine mesh strainer after 15 minutes and rinse with cold water until it runs clean.
3. Heat the oil or ghee in a medium pot over medium-low heat.
4. Add the cumin seeds carefully and allow them to cook for about a minute before the seeds begin to brown and become fragrant. Add the ground turmeric and ginger.
5. Into the pot , add the rice and dal mixture. Using sea salt and black pepper to season. Stir the 4 cups of water and add them.
6. To bring the mixture to a gentle boil, raise the heat to medium-high. Turn the heat down to a gentle simmer immediately. Simmer for 30 minutes, uncovered, until you get a porridge-like consistency, stirring occasionally. It should be creamy and smooth.
7. To make sure that the texture is smooth, taste the kitchari. If not, you will need a little longer to let it cook.
8. Turn the heat off and, if needed, change the seasoning and stir again. Serve or cool down completely and refrigerate for 3 days in a sealed bottle.

Spring Onion Pancakes

 10 servings 60 minutes 🍲 40 minutes

Ingredients

2 cups (300g) of plain flour, plus extra, to dust
¾ cup of vegetable oil
2 spring onions, thinly sliced

SAUCE

¼ cup Chinese black vinegar
¼ cup of soy sauce
2 tsp caster sugar
1 tsp sesame oil
2 long sliced red chillies

1. Sift the flour with a pinch of salt into a large tub. In the middle, build a well and add 160 ml of lukewarm water. Draw in the flour with your fingertips, working from the middle outwards until the dough all comes together. Turn out and knead for 6 minutes or until smooth and elastic on a clean work surface. Drizzle in a clean bowl with 60 ml of vegetable oil and apply the dough, turning to coat thoroughly. Set aside to rest at room temp. For 1 hour.
2. Meanwhile, mix all the ingredients in a small bowl, stir to dissolve the sugar, and set aside to make the dipping sauce.
3. Remove the dough from the oil and cut it into ten pieces.
4. Roll out one piece to a 15-cm round on a lightly floured work surface. Spread with a pinch of salt and 1 tbsp of spring onions. Spray with vegetable oil. To enclose the onion, roll up the dough, coil it into a round disk, and press down to seal with your palms. Roll out to a 15 cm round once again using a lightly floured rolling pin. Place and set aside on a sheet of baking paper. To build ten pancakes, repeat with the remaining dough, oil, and spring onions.
5. Heat half the remaining oil over medium to high heat in a big, non-stick frying pan. Working in lots, cook pancakes, turning each side for 2 minutes or until golden and flaky, adding more oil as needed to the pan. Put on a towel paper to absorb the excess oil, then cut into wedges and serve immediately with dipping sauce, extra spring onions and chili.

Healthy Pumpkin Waffles

🍴 4 servings   🥣 10 minutes   🍲 6 minutes

Ingredients

2 tbsps of unsalted butter
pure pumpkin puree canned (1 cup)
3 large eggs
2 tbsps of pure maple syrup or honey
1 tsp of vanilla extract
2 3/4 of cups milk
2 tsps of ground cinnamon

1 tsp of allspice
1/2 tsp of ground nutmeg
1/4 tsp of ground cloves
2 tsps of baking powder
1 tsp of baking soda
1/2 tsp of salt
2 1/2 cups of whole wheat white flour

Directions

1. Preheat waffle iron.
2. To melt the butter, put the butter in a large bowl and heat it in the microwave.
3. To mix, add the pumpkin puree and whisk.
4. To mix, add the eggs, maple syrup or honey, and vanilla and whisk.
5. Whisk the milk in it.
6. Connect the cinnamon, herbs, nutmeg, cloves, baking powder, salt, and baking soda. Whisk before combined well.
7. Whisk the whole wheat flour white.
8. Cook waffles in a greased, preheated waffle iron according to the directions of the maker.
9. Take mine for 6 minutes per waffle.
10. It freezes waffles well. To cool, move the extra cooked waffles to a wire rack. When cooled, store up to 3 months of waffles in a zip-top bag in the freezer.
11. Defrost and then warm/crisp gently on low heat in a toaster or oven.

Tasty to eat
Revitalizing
Time

Pomegranate, Arugula Salad

🍴 4 servings   🥗 5 minutes   🍲 0 minutes

Ingredients

1/4 cup of pomegranate molasses
1/2 juiced lemon
2 tbsps of honey
2 tbsps of red wine vinegar
3/4 cup of olive oil
black pepper and Kosher salt
6 cups lightly packed arugula
1 pomegranate, seeds only
1/4 cup of Parmigiano
1/4 cup of toasted walnuts
1 sliced shallot

Directions

1. Combine the molasses, lemon juice, honey, and vinegar in a mixing bowl and whisk together to make a vinaigrette. Slowly drizzle in the olive oil thus emulsifying the whisk. Season with salt and pepper.
2. Toss together the salad ingredients and dress them with a vinaigrette.

Peas Pulao with Basmati Rice

 4 servings   10 minutes 20minutes

Ingredients

2 tbsps of GrapeOla Grape Seed oil
1 diced medium onion
2 tsps minced garlic
1 tsp minced ginger
1 green sliced lengthwise chili
1 cup of green peas
¼ cup of toasted cashews
2 tbsps of chopped fresh mint
1 cup of Royal Basmati Rice
1 ¾ cups of water
1 star anise
1 cinnamon stick
3 green cardamom pods
2 tsps of cumin seeds
1 bay leaf
Salt and pepper

Directions

1. Heat oil over medium heat in a medium saute pan with a close-fitting lid.
2. Add the onion and sauté until soft, 3 to 5 minutes.
3. To combine, add garlic, ginger, chili, peas, and cashews and stir.
4. Mint, rice, water, and spices are added. Just bring it to a boil. Cook for 15 minutes or until water is absorbed.
5. Reduce heat to boil and cover.

Spicy Black Bean Soup

🍴 6 servings   🥣 10 minutes   🍲 45 minutes

Ingredients

2 tbsps of extra-virgin olive oil
2 medium chopped yellow onions
3 finely chopped celery ribs
1 large carrot, peeled and slice
into thin rounds
6 pressed or minced garlic cloves
4 ½ tsps of ground cumin
½ tsp of red pepper flakes
Rinsed and drained black beans
(4 cans)

4 cups (32 ounces) of low-
sodium vegetable broth
¼ cup of chopped fresh cilantro
1 to 2 tsps of sherry vinegar
Salt from the sea and freshly
ground black pepper
Optional garnishes: diced
avocado, extra cilantro, thinly
sliced radishes, tortilla chips

Directions

1. In a big soup pot over medium heat or a Dutch oven, heat the olive oil. Sprinkle the onions, celery, and carrots, and salt gently. Cook, occasionally stirring, for about 10 to 15 minutes, until the vegetables are soft.
2. Over a medium-high fire, the beans and broth are brought to a boil. Stir in the flakes of garlic, cumin, and red pepper and cook for around 30 seconds, until fragrant.
3. Cook until the broth is flavored and the beans are very tender for about 30 minutes, decreasing the heat required to maintain a gentle simmer.
4. Move about 4 cups of soup to a blender, tie the icing tightly and mix until smooth (never fill the blender to the highest filling line and be careful not to steam from the top of the blender). For blending, use an immersion blender.
5. Stir in the coriander leaves, vinegar/lime juice, and salt and pepper to taste. Return the powdered soup to the pot. Just serve.

Fava Bean Soup with Lentils

 4 servings   15 minutes   45 minutes

Ingredients

3 tbsps of olive oil
1 tsp of black pepper
½ tsp of red pepper flakes
5 chopped cloves garlic
1 large whole diced onion
3 sprigs thyme
2 tbsps of tomato paste
1 pound of dry baby green lentils
3 diced carrots finely

3 finely diced stalks celery
8 cups of vegetable stock
1 28 ounce can crushed tomatoes
½ cup of Chianti wine optional
2 cups of water
3 14 ounce cans fava beans
1 tbsp of dried oregano
1 bay leaf

Directions

1. The canned fava beans are drained, washed, and shelled. Attach the last bean and pinch. Toss of skin
2. Fry the olive oil, red and black pepper, garlic, onion, and until flavored in a big Dutch oven in a baking oven. Attach the carrots, celery, and thyme and cook until the onions caramelize for another 10 minutes.
3. Attach the paste of the tomatoes and blend until mixed.
4. Stir in the pulses, vegetable stock, tomatoes, oregano and bay leaves, wine (if used). If required, add more water to cover all the ingredients. At low temperatures
5. Cover them occasionally and cook for 30 minutes.
6. Add the fava beans and more water if the broth needs the desired thinning or concentration. Attach it if your permission has been extended. For another 10-15 minutes, cook the lentils and fava beans until hot. Spread bay leaves before serving.
7. Serve with toasted bread with garlic and perm cheese.

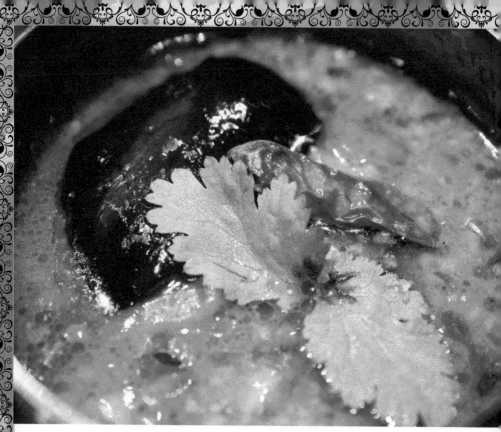

Roasted Eggplant Curry

🍴 6 servings   🥣 15 minutes   🍲 70 minutes

Ingredients

2 3 medium eggplants
¼ cup of olive oil
sea salt
½ tsp of freshly ground
pepper
¼ cup of coconut oil
½ medium chopped white
onion
1 tsp of chili powder
2 tsps of ground cardamom
1 tsp of smoked paprika

1 tsp of ground coriander
1 tbsp of ground turmeric
3 minced cloves garlic
1 tsp of minced ginger and
peeled
3 roma tomatoes, Ripe scliced
into Medium size
15 oz of coconut milk
½ cup of water
cooked rice
chopped fresh cilantro

Directions

- Preheat your oven to 392 degrees Fahrenheit.
- Slice the tops off the eggplants, then lengthwise slice them in half.
- Split each half of it lengthwise once more.
- On their smooth sides, lie the slices and cut them into thirds lengthwise.
- Finally, slice to form cubes horizontally.
- Drizzle with olive oil, salt, and pepper on a baking sheet.
- Bake until golden brown for 25 minutes, stirring halfway through.
- Heat the coconut oil over a tall hat in a large saucepan.
- Add the onions, stir for 1 minute, then will the heat to medium-low and cook until the onions are golden brown, stirring occasionally, for about 8 minutes.
- Stir in the chili powder, cardamom, and smoked paprika.
- Cook until fragrant, about 1 minute.
- Stir in the ground coriander, ½ tsp of black pepper, turmeric, garlic, and ginger.
- Cook for a few minutes more, stirring constantly.
- Add the chopped tomatoes, coconut milk, water, and roasted eggplant.
- Bring the curry to a simmer, then reduce to low heat, cover, and simmer for 25 minutes. The sauce should reduce and thicken slightly.
- Serve the curry warm over rice, topped with chopped cilantro.
- Enjoy!

White Bean Kale and Artichoke Dip

 2 servings   15 minutes   🍲 30 minutes

Ingredients

FOR THE DIP

1 tsp of olive oil
2 minced garlic cloves
6 cups of fresh baby kale
6 drained and chopped
artichoke hearts
1 15 oz of white beans
drained and rinsed
1 T lemon juice

1/2 cup of 0% plain greek yogurt
1/2 cup of unsweetened almond milk
1 T of dijon mustard
salt and pepper
1/4 parmesan cheese

FOR THE FLATBREAD

1 cup of quinoa flour
3 T of ground flaxseed
1/2 tsp of sea salt
1 cup of water

FOR THE DIP

1. In a large pot, boil water.
2. Let the water boil once and cook for 30-45 seconds or until it is over.
3. Drain and cover with cold water right away. Turn the water off and drain completely when the cal has cooled.
4. Using a dish rag or paper towel to remove all moisture from the cow. It would help if you had a ball at the end, which is 2/3 of the cup.
5. Cut into tiny pieces.
6. Combine the white beans, lemon juice, Greek yogurt, almond milk, and mustard in a food processor blender. Process the mixture until it is smooth (about 1-2 minutes). Only set aside.
7. Over medium heat, heat the olive oil in a large pot.
8. Add in the garlic and kale, then cook for 1 minute.
9. Add in the artichokes and quit for a minute.
10. To the puree, add the dried beans and reduce the heat to medium-low. It will begin to bubble and thicken the mixture. Stir occasionaly for 3-5 minutes or until you have achieved the desired consistency.
11. Stir the cheese in.
12. With flatbread and/or veggies, serve soft.
13. For up to five days, refrigerate.

FOR THE FLATBREAD

1. Preheat the oven to 204.444°C and 400°F.
2. Mix the dry ingredients.
3. Stir in water until you create a thick batter.
4. Line a silicone mat or parchment paper with a baking sheet.
5. Scoop each side of the baking sheet with a 1/4 cup of batter (2 flatbreads per sheet).
6. Use a spatula to spread the mixture until it's a 1/4 inch thick medium-sized circle (about 6 inches).
7. Bake for about 12 mins.
8. Remove from the oven and let the sheet cool for 5 mins.
9. Take it off the sheet and cut it into four triangles.
10. Send the triangles back to the baking sheet and bake for another five minutes.
11. Serve warm or let sit and firm up to cool down.

Lentil and Cauliflower Curry

🍴 4 servings   🥣 10 minutes   🍲 35 minutes

Ingredients

1 tbsp o folive oil
1 large chopped onion
3 tbsp of curry paste
1 tsp of turmeric
1 tsp of mustard seeds
200g of red or yellow lentil
1l low-sodium vegetable or chicken stock
1 large cauliflower, broken into florets
1 large diced potato
3 tbsp of coconut yogurt
small pack chopped coriander
juice 1 lemon
100g of cooked brown rice

Directions

1. In a large saucepan, heat the oil and cook until the onion is soft, leave with curry paste, spices, and lentils for about five minutes and stir with the onion and lentils to make the onion and onion.
2. Top with stock and cook for 20 minutes. If it looks a little dry, add cauliflower, potatoes, and some water.
3. For about 12 minutes, boil the cauliflower and potatoes until smooth. Stir in the yogurt, lemon juice, and coriander and serve with brown rice.

Creamy Roasted Carrot Soup

 4 servings   15 minutes   50 minutes

Ingredients

2 pounds of carrots

3 tbsps of extra-virgin divided olive oil

¾ tsp of fine sea salt

1 medium of yellow chopped onion

2 cloves pressed or minced garlic

½ tsp of ground coriander

¼ tsp of ground cumin

4 cups of vegetable broth

2 cups of water

Unsalted butter of 1-2 tbsps

1 ½ tsps of lemon juice

Freshly ground black pepper

Directions

1. Preheat the oven to 400 degrees Fahrenheit.
2. To prepare your carrots, peel them and then cut them on the diagonal so each piece is about ½" thick at the widest part.
3. Place the carrots on the baking sheet. Add 2 tablespoons olive oil and ½ teaspoon of salt. Toss until the carrots are lightly coated in oil and seasonings. Arrange them in a single layer.
4. Roast the carrots until they're caramelized on the edges and easily pierced through by a fork, 25 to 40 minutes, tossing halfway.
5. Once the carrots are almost done roasting, warm the remaining 1 tablespoon olive oil over medium heat until shimmering in a Dutch oven or soup pot.
6. Add the onion and ¼ teaspoon salt.
7. Cook, occasionally stirring until the onion is softened and turning translucent, 5 to 7 minutes.
8. Add the garlic, coriander, and cumin. Cook until fragrant while constantly stirring, about 30 seconds to 1 minute.
9. Pour in the vegetable broth and water while scraping up any browned bits on the bottom with a wooden spoon or sturdy silicone spatula.
10. Add the roasted carrots to the pot when they are out of the oven.
11. Bring the mixture to a boil over high heat, then reduce the heat as necessary to maintain a gentle simmer.
12. Cook for 15 minutes to give the flavors time to meld.
13. Once the soup is done cooking, remove the pot from the heat and let it cool for a few minutes. Then, carefully transfer the hot soup to a blender, working in batches if necessary.
14. Add the butter, lemon juice, and several twists of black pepper. Blend until completely smooth.
15. Add additional salt and pepper, if necessary, to taste.
16. Add another tablespoon of butter if you'd like more richness or a little more lemon juice if it needs more zing.
17. Blend again, and serve.

This soup keeps well in the refrigerator, covered, for about four days or several months in the freezer.

Red Lentil-Pumpkin Soup

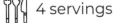 4 servings 10 minutes 30 minutes

Ingredients

- Olive oil spray
- 1 brown onion, finely chopped
- 2 garlic cloves, crushed
- 1 tsp finely grated fresh ginger
- 2 tsp curry powder
- 1kg butternut pumpkin, peeled, deseeded, cut into 1cm-pieces

- 175g (3/4 cup) red lentils, rinsed
- 1.25L (5 cups) water
- 1 Massel vegetable stock cube
- 90g (1/3 cup) low-fat natural yoghurt
- Fresh coriander leaves, to serve

Directions

1. Heat a large saucepan over medium-low heat. Spray with olive oil spray
2. Click on the underlined ingredient to reveal the quantity. No need to flip back and forth!
3. Add the onion and cook, for 5 minutes or until soft.
4. Add the garlic, ginger, and curry powder and cook, stirring, for 1 minute or until aromatic.
5. Add the pumpkin, lentils, water and stock cube.
6. Bring to the boil. Reduce heat to low.
7. Simmer, partially covered, for 15-20 minutes or until the pumpkin and lentils are soft. Set aside to cool.
8. Ladle half the lentil mixture into the jug of a blender and blend until smooth. Transfer to a clean saucepan. Repeat with the remaining lentil mixture.
9. Place the soup over medium heat and cook, stirring, for 3 minutes or until heated through.
10. Season with pepper. Ladle among serving bowls.
11. Top with the yoghurt and coriander to serve.

Summer Bean and Herb Pasta

 4 servings　 10 minutes　🍲 15 minutes

Ingredients

400g long pasta (any you have)
Prepared, blanched until tender, then refreshed in cold water, 400 g of green beans.
4 tbsp of olive oil
2 finely chopped, grated, or crushed garlic cloves
zest and juice of 1 lemon
2 handfuls of mixed herbs, chopped
100g Parmesan or grated vegetarian alternative
salt and pepper

Directions

1. In a large pan of salted boiling water, add the pasta and cook according to the instructions on the packet. Set aside a few ladlefuls of the cooking water, and then drain it.
2. Meanwhile, heat the oil in a big frying pan—gently warm the beans, garlic, lemon zest, and juice for 1 minute. Remove yourself from the heat.
3. Add the pasta, three-quarters of the fresh herbs, and half of the grated Parmesan cheese to the frying pan. To mix everything, season with salt and pepper and toss gently.
4. To loosen it up, add some of the reserved pasta water. Pass the pasta and sprinkle over the remaining herbs and parmesan to serve in a large serving dish.

Peanut Butter Banana Shakeology Muffins

🍴 12 servings   🥣 10 minutes   🍲 10 minutes

Ingredients

2 cups oats old fashioned
3/4 cup peanut butter
2 bananas ripe
2 eggs
2 cup greek yogurt plain nonfat
2 tbsp honey
1 tsp vanilla
1 tsp baking powder
1/4 tsp salt
1/2 scoop Shakeology strawberry flavor
1 tsp flax seed powder

Directions

1. Combine 1/2 cup of Greek yogurt with 1/2 cup of peanut butter, rice, bananas, eggs, honey, baking powder, vanilla, and salt in a blender.
2. Pulse until everything's mixed up.
3. Pour into greased tins and bake for 10 minutes at 400. As you whip up the frosting, set the muffins aside to cool.
4. In a mixer, add 1 1/2 cup of Greek yogurt, 3 tbsp peanut butter, 1/2 scoop of Shakeology, and a little flax seed powder and stir until a creamy texture develops.
5. Spread the muffins on top and put them in the fridge!

Herb frittatas

🍴 12 servings   🥣 10 minutes   🍳 30 minutes

Ingredients

12 large eggs
1/2 tsp of salt
1/4 tsp of pepper
3 tbsps of olive oil
1 small chopped onion
1 minced clove garlic
2 tbsps of chopped fresh herbs

Directions

1. Preheat the oven to 350 degrees F.
2. Using cooking spray to coat a 12-cup nonstick muffin tin.
3. Whisk the eggs with salt and pepper in a large bowl until they are combined.
4. Over medium-high heat, melt the oil into a small skillet.
5. Sauté the onion until tender but not browned, for 3 to 5 minutes. Include the garlic and sauté for another 1 minute.
6. Remove and cool slightly from the sun.
7. Whisk the herbs and onion mixture into the eggs.
8. Divide between the 12 cups of muffin and bake for 25 to 30 minutes until set in the middle.

Sweet Fried Semolina Pudding

 4 servings   35 minutes   45 minutes

Ingredients

200 g semolina
1 l milk
80 g sugar
1 tsp of vanilla extract
50 g wheat flour
2 pieces eggs
100 ml of sunflower oil

Directions

1. I put the milk, along with vanilla and 80 g of sugar, in a pot to boil.
2. Slowly pour the semolina over the milk as it starts to boil, mixing it with an egg beater.
3. Boil over medium-low heat for 10 minutes, stirring continuously, until the pudding thickens.
4. Pour it on a plate, or on any flat surface, when the pudding is ready. Spread the pudding uniformly in the thickness of 1 cm-1.5 cm with a spatula as you wish and let it cool.
5. Break the pudding with a knife into roughly similar shapes after it has cooled.
6. Put about 50 g of wheat flour on a plate, through which we pass the pieces of pudding.
7. Beat two whole eggs well in a bowl and push through the bits of pudding we've shaken out of the flour.
8. Heat 100 ml of sunflower oil in a pan, then fry the pudding in it. Fry them for around 2-3 minutes, on each side, on medium heat, until they turn golden.
9. On a kitchen towel, remove the fried semolina pudding slices and let them drain away from the oil.

Baked Flageolet Beans with Ham

🍴 4 servings　　🥣 20 minutes　　🍲 5 minutes

Ingredients

2 cups of flageolet beans	4 cups of chicken
2-3 tbsp of olive oil	2 bay leaves
1 cup of diced ham	2 tbsp of fresh thyme
2 cups of diced onion	2 cups of water
3 medium-sized diced carrots	salt and pepper
4 minced cloves of garlic	

Directions

1. Cover the dried beans, cover the bowl with water, and refrigerate overnight. The water above the beans should be about an inch.
2. Preheat the oven to 300 degrees the next day.
3. Drain the beans and rinse them.
4. Heat the olive oil in a big ovenproof pot over medium heat.
5. Add the diced ham, onions and carrots. The vegetables should be soft but not browned and cook for 7-8 minutes. For 1 minute stir in the garlic and saute. (Careful that the garlic does not overcook.)
6. To the pot, add the beans, broth, bay leaves and thyme. For 45 minutes cover and bake it in the oven.
7. Remove and reveal it from the oven.
8. To taste, apply salt and pepper. Boost the temperature to 350 degrees and cook in the oven for an extra 45-60 minutes. If the beans seem to dry at any point, stir in more water or broth up to 2 cups-and allow them to continue to cook until tender.
9. The beans should be tender, and the pan will contain a small amount of liquid. Remove the leaves from the bay and serve sweet!

Creamy Lemon Rice

🍴 4 servings 🍚 5 minutes 🍲 15 minutes

Ingredients

2-1/2 cups of chicken broth
2 ounces cubed cream cheese
1/2 tsp of grated lemon zest
1 tbsp of lemon juice
1/4 tsp of salt
1/4 tsp of coarsely ground pepper
Long grain rice uncooked (1 cup)
1/4 of cup minced fresh basil

Directions

1. Combine the first six ingredients in a casserole; bring to a boil.
2. To mix, stir with a whisk.
3. Incorporate rice; return to a boil. Reduce heat;
4. Simmer
5. Cover until rice is tender and liquid is absorbed around 15 minutes.
6. Stir the basil in.

Tofu Tacos

 6 servings    5 minutes   15 minutes

Ingredients

Vegetable broth (¼ cup)
1 chopped small onion
1/2 small seeded and cutted into cubs bell pepper
1 cup of firm, shredded tofu
1 tbsp of chili powder
1 tbsp of nutritional yeast
1 tsp of garlic powder
1/4 tsp of ground cumin

1/4 tsp of dried oregano
1 tbsp of soy sauce
6 corn tortillas
1 cup of julienned lettuce
2 chopped green onions
1/2 cup of chopped tomato
1/3 cup salsa
1/2 sliced avocado

Directions

1. In a non-stick pan, heat water or vegetable stock.
2. Add the onion and red pepper and cook, frequently stirring, over high heat, for 2 to 3 minutes.
3. Add tofu, chili powder, garlic powder, cumin, oregano, and soy sauce, nutritional yeast (if used).
4. Reduce the heat to medium and simmer for 3 minutes, stirring frequently.
5. In a dry, heavy pan, heat the tortilla, rotating it from side to side until soft and flexible.
6. In the middle, put a small amount of tofu mixture, fold the tortilla in half and remove it from the sun.
7. Garnish, if using, with lettuce, green onions, tomatoes, sauce, and avocado.
8. For each remaining tortilla, repeat.

Sweet Potatoes Buddha Bowls

 2 servings   20 minutes   🍲 30 minutes

Ingredients

SWEET POTATO AND ONIONS

2 large(4 cups chopped) sweet potatoes, chopped into cubes
1 large chopped red onion
2 tbsps of olive oil
2 tsps of garlic powder
1 tsp of curry powder
1 tsp of ground cumin
salt and pepper

FOR THE QUINOA

1 cup of uncooked quinoa
2 cups of water

KALE AND BRUSSELS

1-2 tbsps of olive oil
1 tbsp of minced garlic
4 cups of kale
2 cups of shaved Brussels sprouts
salt and pepper

Directions

SWEET POTATOES AND ONIONS

1. Preheat your oven to 400oF and spray with cooking spray on a baking sheet or rub with olive oil.
2. Place the vegetables and drizzle with the olive oil on the baking sheet.
3. Sprinkle with spices. You can use your hands to rub the spices into the vegetables.
4. Bake for 25-30 minutes at 400 degrees F.

QUINOA

1. Prepare your quinoa while your veggies are cooking.
2. Then bring the quinoa and water to a boil in a medium pot. Cover and switch to low heat and boil, covered, for about 15-20 minutes or until all the water has evaporated.

KALE AND BRUSSELS

1. Heat a large skillet in high heat. Add olive oil.
2. Add garlic when the olive oil is fragrant.
3. In the pan, add the kale and Brussels and saute for 5-7 minutes. Take the heat off and season with salt and pepper.

FOR THE BUDDHA BOWLS

1. Separate the mixture of quinoa, sweet potatoes, and kale uniformly into six bowls or containers for meal prep.
2. Top with tahini (or any of your choice of salad dressing or hummus) and sesame seeds, and enjoy!

Brussels Sprout Soup

🍴 4 servings   🥣 10 minutes   🍲 21 minutes

Ingredients

400g brussel sprouts
1 chopped onion
2 cloves garlic
750ml vegetable stock
Cheddar cheese

Directions

IN A SOUP MAKER

1. Optional: saute the garlic and onions.
2. Add all the ingredients to the soup maker, except for the cheese.
3. Start yourself off smoothly.
4. Add a little grated cheese and let it melt (optional).

IN A SAUCEPAN

1. In a bit of butter or oil, saute the onions and garlic.
2. Cook for approximately 5 minutes, or until the onion turns light brown.
3. Chop the Brussel sprouts and return them to the plate.
4. For a further 2 to 3 minutes, cook gently.
5. Connect to the stock of vegetables and bring to a boil.
6. Reduce heat and simmer until sprouts are tender, or for 15 to 20 minutes.
7. Blitz until smooth (you might need to leave the soup to cool a bit before blending) using a hand blender.
8. Incorporate grated cheese (optional).

Rice, Lentil Porridge

 6 servings    10 minutes   20 minutes

Ingredients

3/4 cups of yellow or red lentils
2/3 cup of Basmati Rice
1 tsp of ghee
2 tsps of black mustard seeds
1 tsp of fenugreek seeds
1/8 tsp of asafoetida
1 tbsp of minced ginger

1 tsp of turmeric
1 tsp of cumin
2 bay leaves
4 cups of water
Cilantro
Yogurt
Salt and pepper

Directions

1. Heat the ghee over medium heat in a 3-quart-large pot with a lid.
2. Until the mustard seeds pop, add mustard and fenugreek seeds and toast.
3. Stir in asafoetida, ginger, turmeric, and cumin and simmer for 30 seconds.
4. Attach the Basmati Rice lentils and stir until coated with spices.
5. Add water to the pot and add bay leaves and bring to a boil: cover and boil. For 15-20 minutes, cook.
6. By adding more water, you can thin the khichdi to the desired consistency. With salt and pepper, season.
7. Using yogurt and cilantro to serve.

Mushroom Rice

 6 servings    15 minutes   25 minutes

Ingredients

2 cups of cooked rice

400 grams of white button mushrooms

Virgin olive oil extra (2 tbsps)

1 tsp of roasted crushed sesame seeds

½ tsp of thyme

½ tsp of oregano

3 to 4 spring chopped onions or scallions

1 tsp of finely chopped garlic

¼ tsp of black pepper powder or white pepper powder

salt

Directions

1. Heat the olive oil in the pan.
2. Add the garlic that has been sliced. Sauté for a couple of seconds.
3. Then add 3-4 (spring onion whites) chopped small to medium scallions. Start with the spring onions to saute.
4. Saute until they become translucent with the spring onions. Now add 400 grams of mushrooms, chopped.
5. Saute the mushrooms until they leave the water and are thoroughly dried and baked.
6. Connect to the mushrooms the black or white pepper, crushed sesame seeds, thyme, and oregano. Mix thoroughly.
7. Now add the rice and salt that has been cooked.
8. Saute the rice for a couple of minutes with the mushrooms.
9. Garnish it with green scallions.
10. Serve hot with a salad, or just drizzle the rice with some extra virgin olive oil and enjoy the mushroom rice bowl.

Vegetarian Kale Soup

 8 servings   25 minutes   30 minutes

Ingredients

2 tbsps of olive oil
1 yellow chopped onion
2 tbsps of chopped garlic
1 stems removed and leaves chopped bunch kale,
8 cups of water
6 cubes vegetable bouillon
1 can diced tomatoes
6 medium peeled and cubed white potatoes
2 (15 ounce) cans cannellini beans
1 tbsp of Italian seasoning
2 tbsps of dried parsley
salt and pepper

Directions

1. In a large soup pot, heat the olive oil; cook the onion and garlic until tender.
2. Stir in the kale and cook for about 2 minutes, until wilted. Add the water, the bouillon of onions, the tomatoes, the potatoes, the beans, the Italian seasoning, and the parsley.
3. Simmer the soup for 25 minutes on medium heat or until the potatoes are thoroughly cooked.
4. Season with salt and pepper for taste.

Summer Vegetable Ratatouille

 8 servings   25 minutes   30 minutes

Ingredients

2 medium onion
3 minced cloves garlic
1 medium cubed eggplant
2 medium cubed zucchini
2 medium cubed yellow squash
2 medium seeded and cubed green bell peppers
1 yellow diced bell pepper
1 chopped red bell pepper

4 plum tomato chopped roma tomatoes
½ cup of olive oil
1 bay leaf
2 tbsps of chopped fresh parsley
4 sprigs fresh thyme
salt and pepper

Directions

1. Heat 1 1/2 tbsps of the oil over medium-low heat in a large pot. Add the garlic and onions and cook until prepare.

2. Heat 1 1/2 tbsps of olive oil in a large skillet and saute the zucchini in batches until lightly browned on all sides.

3. Remove the zucchini and put the onions and garlic in the pot.

4. Saute all the remaining vegetables one batch at a time, and each time you add a new collection of vegetables, add 1 1/2 tbsp of olive oil to the skillet. Add the vegetables to the large pot once each batch has been sauteed.

5. With salt and pepper, season. The bay leaf and thyme are added, and the pot is sealed. For 15 to 20 minutes, cook over medium heat.

6. Add the chopped tomatoes and parsley to a large pot and cook for another 10-15 minutes. Occasionally stir.

7. Change the seasoning and remove the bay leaf.

Carrots and Figs

🍴 8 servings   🥣 25 minutes   🍲 30 minutes

Ingredients

¼ cup of slivered almonds
4 tsps of sugar
½ tsp of grated orange peel
1 pound carrots
½ cup of dried figs, cutted into fourths
1 tbsp of softened butter or margarine

Directions

1. In an 8-inch skillet over low heat, cook the almonds, sugar, and orange peel for about 10 minutes, constantly stirring until the sugar is melted and the almonds are coated; cool. Breakaway the almonds; set aside.
2. In the saucepan, place the steamer basket in 1/2 inch of water (water should not touch the bottom of the basket). Place the carrots in your basket.
3. Tightly cover and heat until boiling; minimize heat.
4. Steam for 9 to 11 minutes or until tender, added for the last 2 minutes with the figs.
5. Toss the almonds and butter with the carrots and figs.

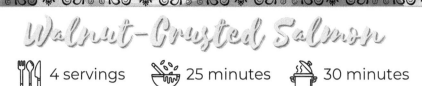

Walnut-Crusted Salmon

🍴 4 servings   🥣 25 minutes   🍲 30 minutes

Ingredients

4 salmon fillets
4 tsps of Dijon mustard
4 tsps of honey
2 slices whole wheat bread
3 tbsps of finely chopped walnuts
2 tsps of canola oil
1/2 tsp of dried thyme

Directions

1. Preheat the oven to 400 degrees.
2. Place salmon coated with cooking spray on a baking sheet. Mix the honey and the mustard; brush over the salmon.
3. In a food processor, place bread; pulse until coarse crumbs develop.
4. Move it to a tiny tub. Stir in the thyme, oil, and walnuts; press on the salmon.
5. Bake 12-15 minutes or until lightly browned topping and fish only begin to easily flake with a fork.

Dedicated to
Your Well-Being

Namastè

Lightning Source UK Ltd.
Milton Keynes UK
UKHW021825090223
416674UK00011B/147